AF419749

AMAZING FACTS ABOUT THE SCIENCE OF SPORTS

SPORTS BOOK GRADE 3

Children's Sports & Outdoors Books

Speedy Publishing LLC

40 E. Main St. #1156

Newark, DE 19711

www.speedypublishing.com

Copyright 2017

Exercising and doing sports is not just fun. It can be great for you! Let's find out what sports science can tell us.

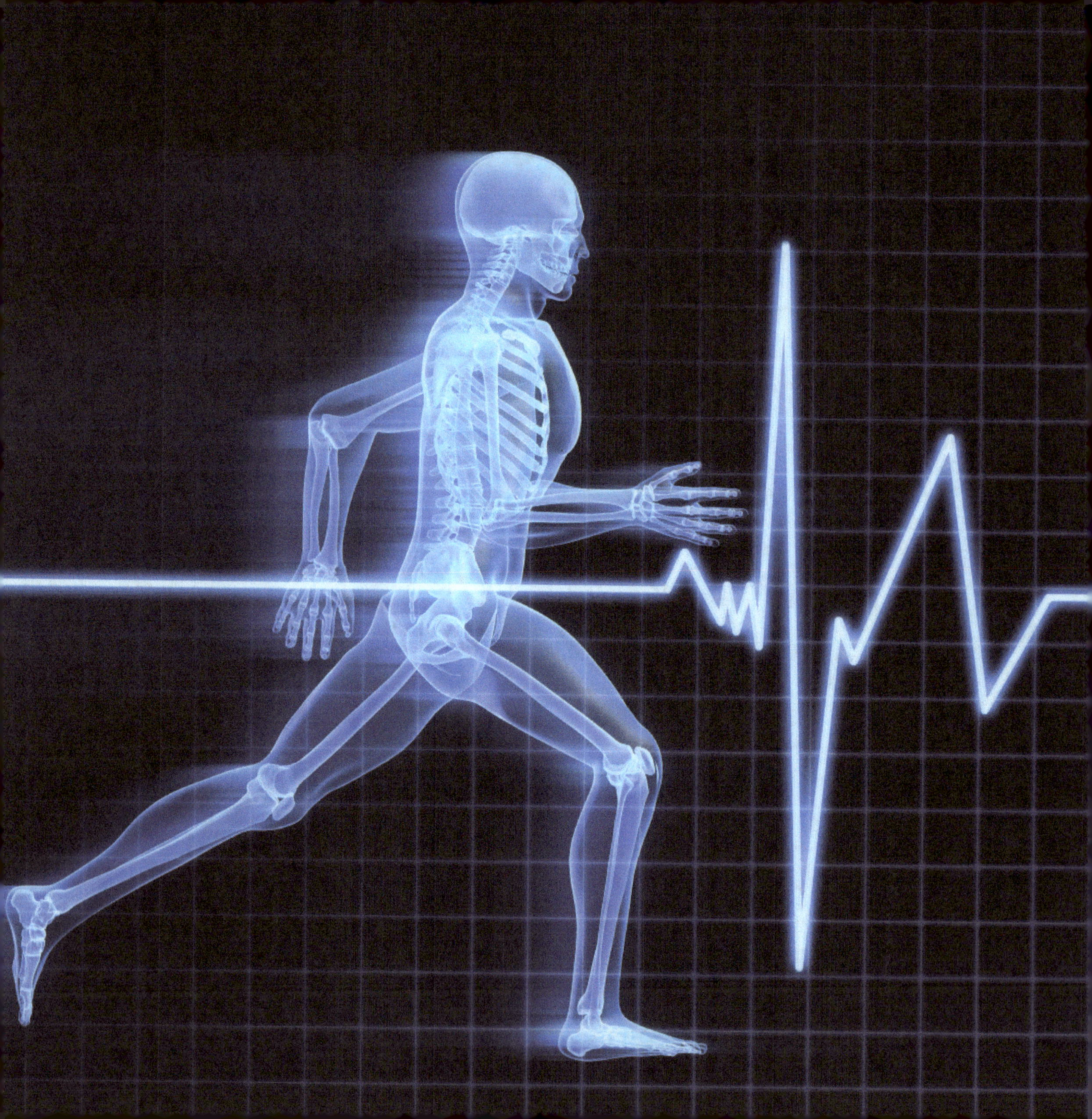

SPORTS AND SCIENCE

There are a lot of doctors, scientists and other specialists who work in "sports science". This field studies how a healthy body does exercise, whether in a game, for work, or just running around for fun.

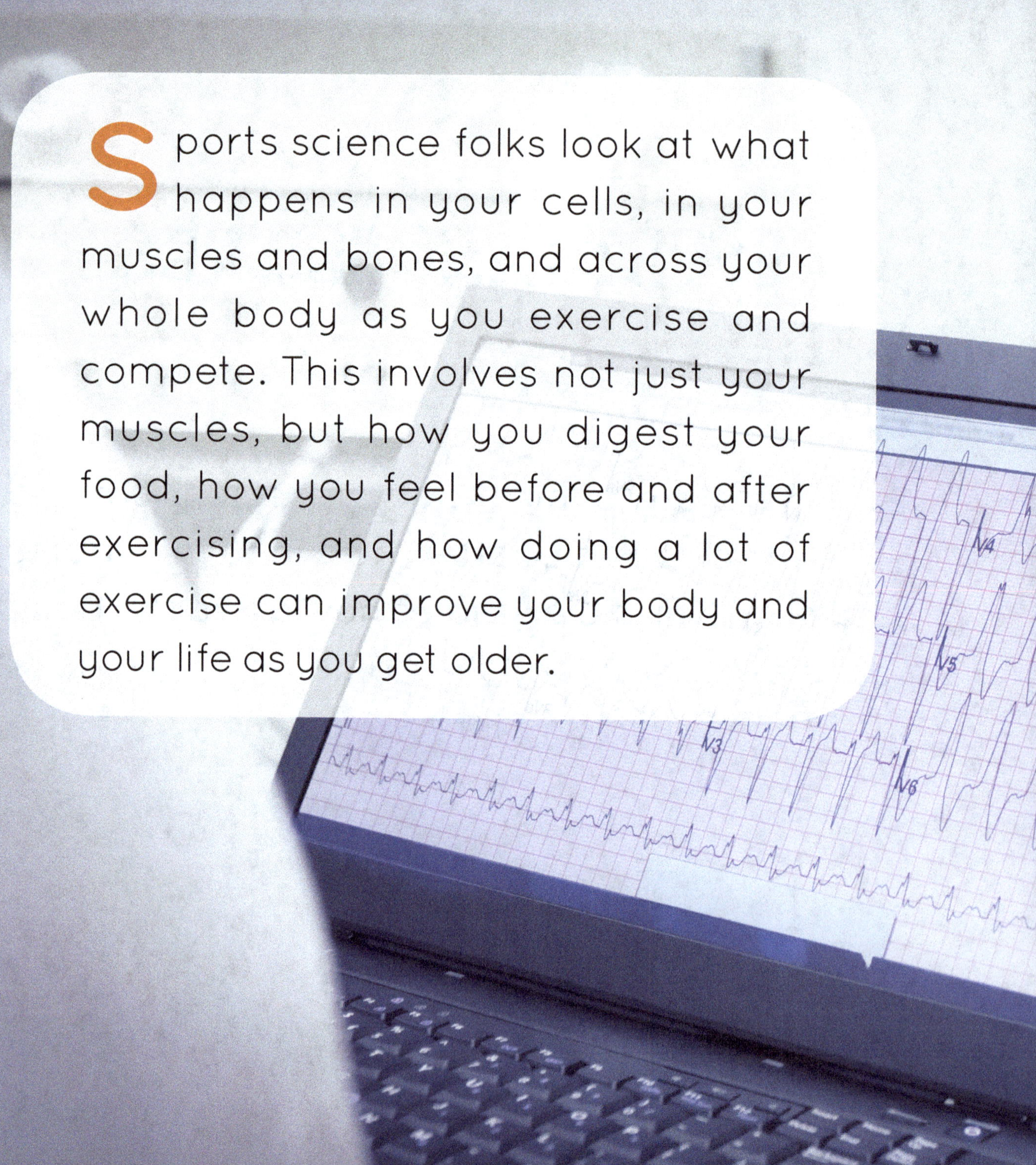

Sports science folks look at what happens in your cells, in your muscles and bones, and across your whole body as you exercise and compete. This involves not just your muscles, but how you digest your food, how you feel before and after exercising, and how doing a lot of exercise can improve your body and your life as you get older.

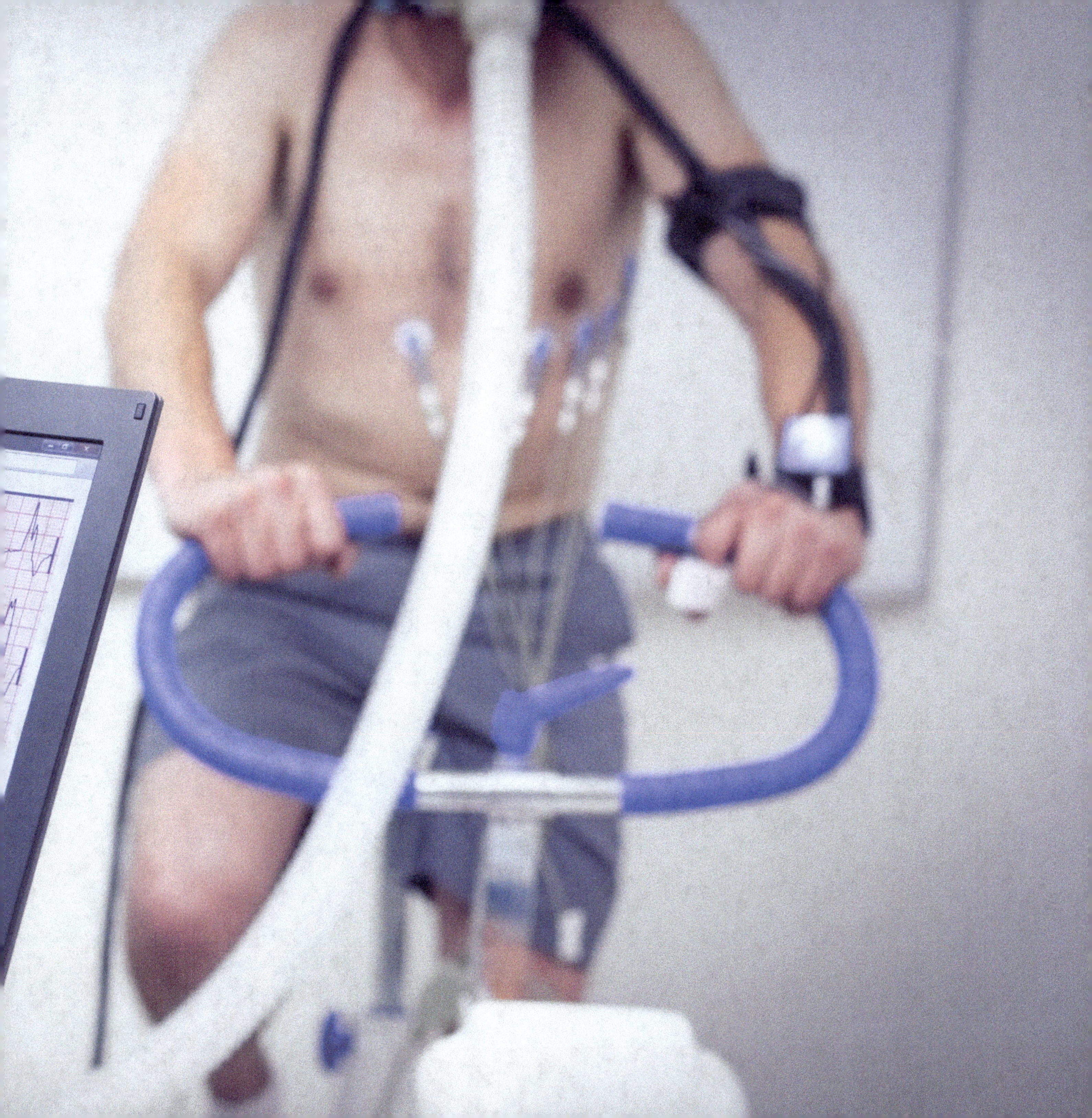

SPORTS AND EXERCISE

You don't have to be on a team in a league to exercise! You can exercise all by yourself, and a lot of people do. They go running, or work out at the gym, or swim laps.

But a lot of people enjoy having a goal. It keeps them interested through all the long days of training when it does not feel like you are getting any stronger or able to run any further than you were before.

AN ATHLETE ON HER STARTING BLOCK

And if you are on a team, wanting to support your team-members and get their approval can encourage you to practice so you can bring your best game on game day.

There are four general areas where sport science concentrates. They are the relation of exercise and sports to:

- Fitness

- Brain activity

- Happiness

- Healing

Let's look at each area.

SPORTS CAN MAKE YOU MORE FIT

Exercise makes you stronger, as your muscle cells become more able to do what you want them to do.

Your body has three types of muscles:

- Smooth muscles mainly support and work with your internal organs.

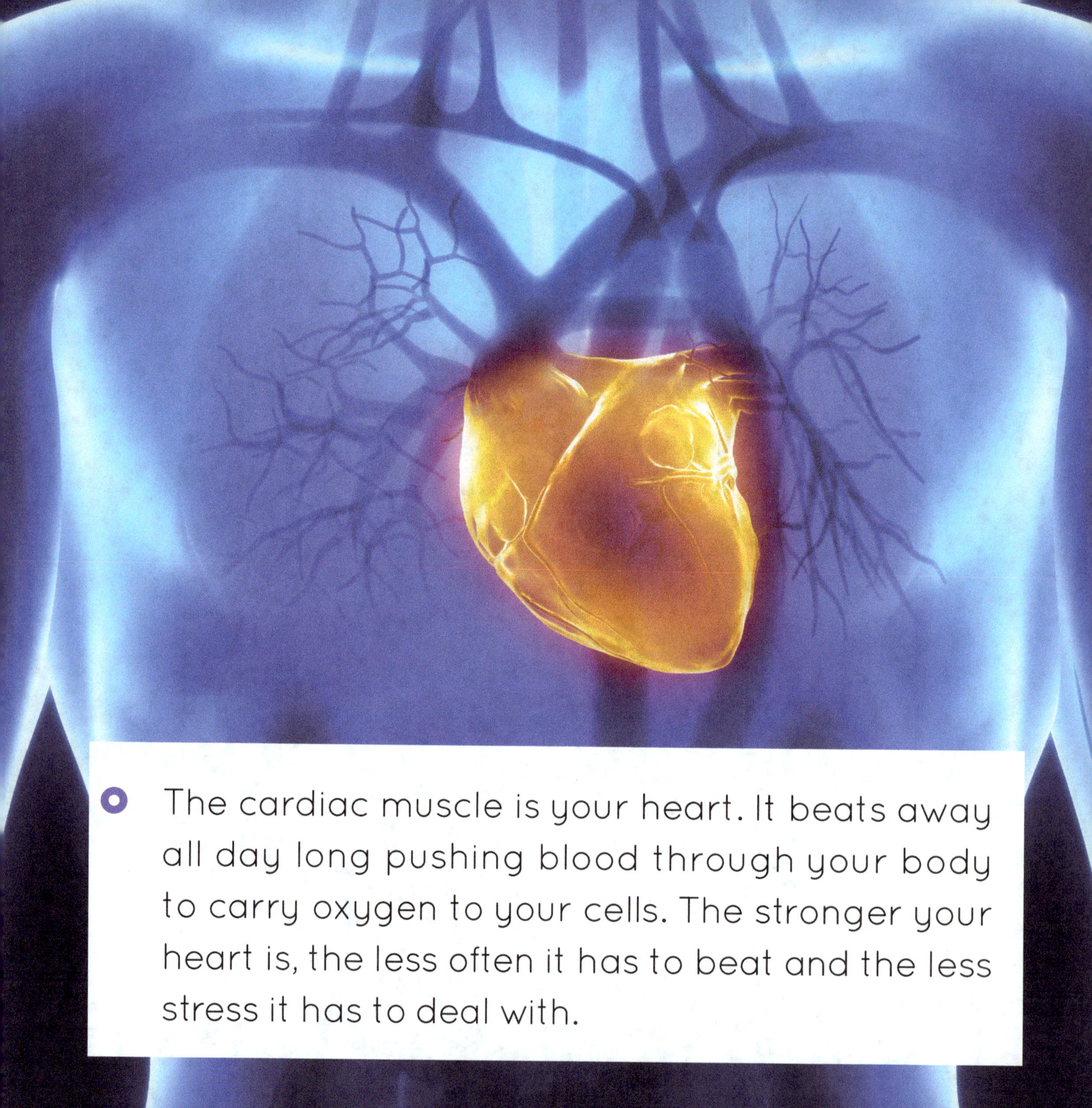

- The cardiac muscle is your heart. It beats away all day long pushing blood through your body to carry oxygen to your cells. The stronger your heart is, the less often it has to beat and the less stress it has to deal with.

- The big muscles in your body, like the biceps in your arms, are skeletal muscles. They attach at each end to bones in your body, and by pulling on those bones help your body move and do things.

Muscle cells have lots of organelles, or mitochondria. These convert glucose (sugar) into a molecule that can store lots of energy that it can quickly release again. This lets your muscles work hard for long periods. Muscle cells have more organelles than other cells in the body.

Most of the volume of skeletal muscles are muscle proteins that help the muscle contract and relax. Sports science people have found that when a person follows a pattern of hard exercise followed by periods of rest, along with a good diet, the muscle protein slowly expands. This makes the muscle able to do more work the next time you call on it.

When you train regularly, you teach your muscle cells to work better together, so they all contract at the same time and give you the full force you need.

SPORTS CAN MAKE YOU SMARTER

When you exercise regularly, it does not just make your body stronger so you can lift weights or run bases. It can also make you smarter!

- You gain both muscle strength and endurance through exercise. This gives your body extra energy, and your brain can use some of that energy. You can think more clearly, and even have better daydreams!

Exercising just thirty minutes a day, according to sports science folks, can greatly improve your thinking ability.

YOGA POSE

- According to researchers, for two or three hours after you exercise you are more able to concentrate and focus on things. Your brain can take in more information, and you can organize and remember more facts more easily. This is because regular exercise improves the blood flow in your brain.

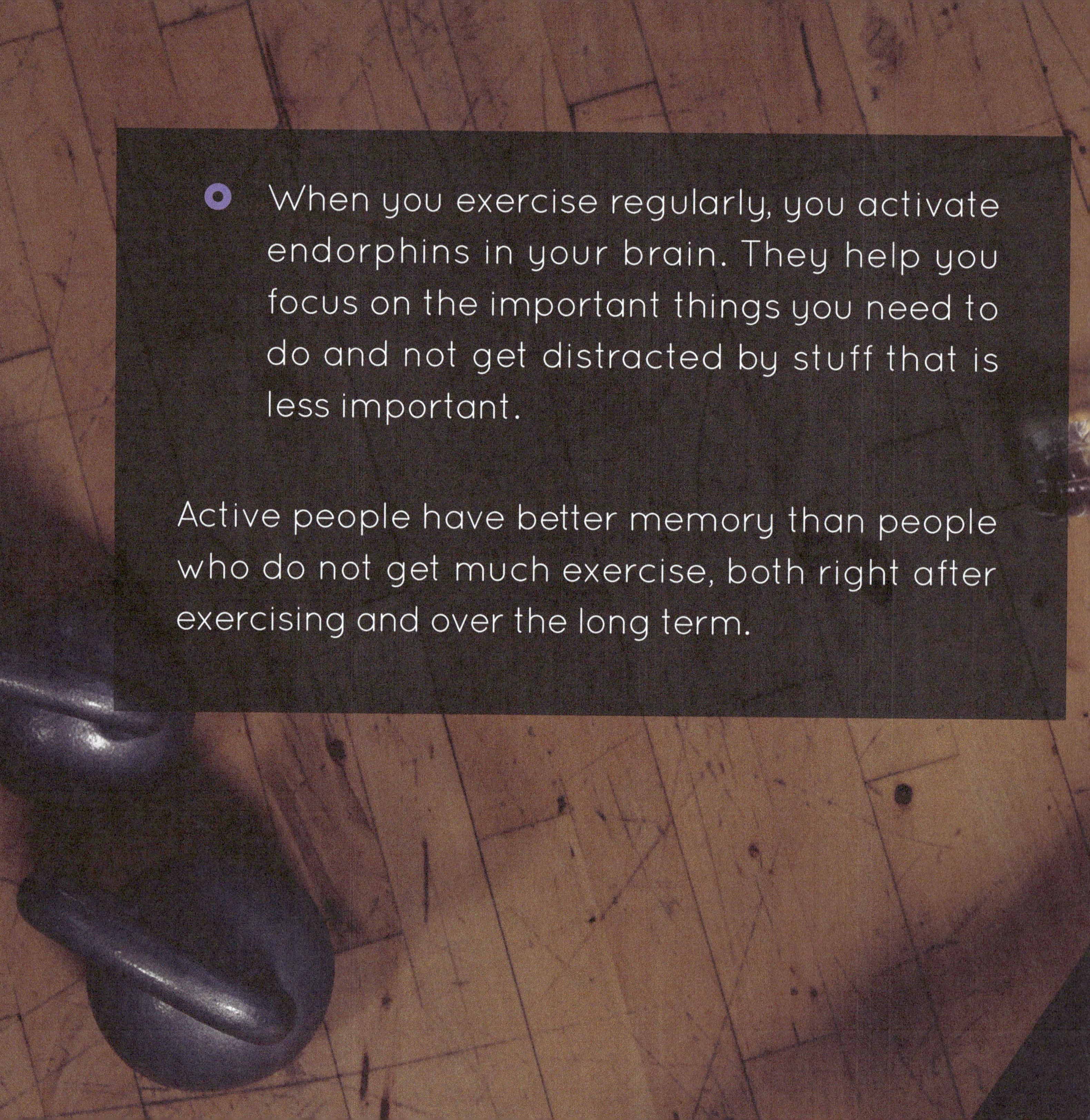

When you exercise regularly, you activate endorphins in your brain. They help you focus on the important things you need to do and not get distracted by stuff that is less important.

Active people have better memory than people who do not get much exercise, both right after exercising and over the long term.

SPORTS CAN MAKE YOU HAPPIER

When you exercise, you release endorphins in your brain. As we said, they help you focus on things better. They are also great at improving your mood and keeping you from getting depressed.

When some people get sad, they need a doctor's prescription for medicine to help their mood. Many other people find that if they start exercising regularly they feel less sad than they used to, without taking any pills!

E ndorphins interact with receptors in your brain. They block some pain signals from getting to the receptors, and they generate positive signals. This can help a person's mood improve.

Runners sometimes find that, on a long run, they suddenly reach a point where everything feels much easier and their body feels great instead of tired.

This is endorphins creating a "runner's high", and it makes the runner's mind feel better and happier, not just the muscles of the body. Regular exercise:

- Reduces stress

- Prevents becoming anxious or worrying too much about minor things

- Helps you feel better about yourself

- Helps you sleep better

INJURED SOCCER PLAYER

HOW TO FIX WHAT GOES WRONG

Along with all the benefits of exercise and playing sports, there is the occasional down-side. Most athletes get injured sometime in their playing career—and even kids playing in the playground can end up getting hurt!

Injuries can happen because:

- You bang into something like a wall, or a thrown baseball hits you.

- You didn't stretch out your muscles before you started running.

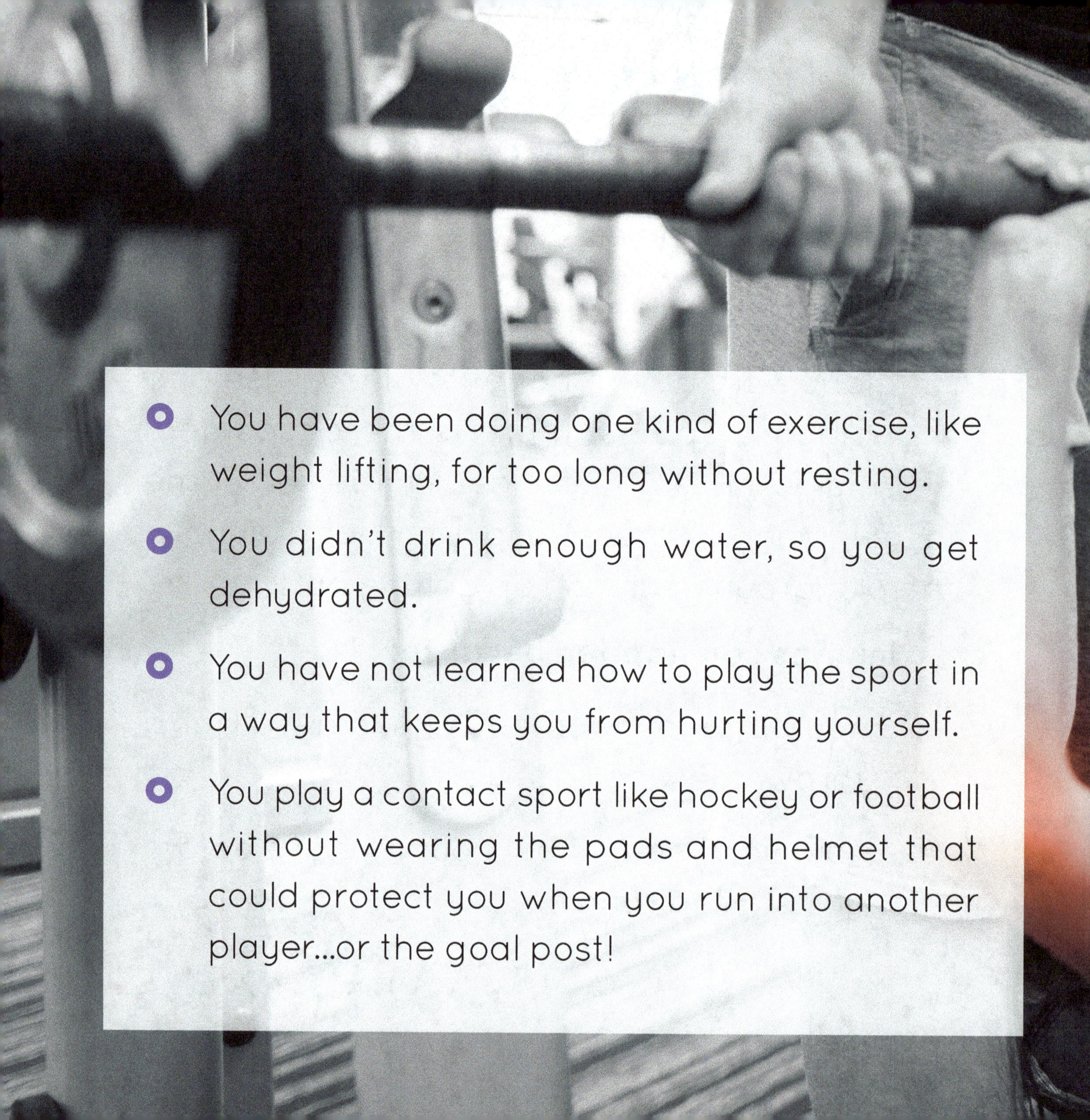

- You have been doing one kind of exercise, like weight lifting, for too long without resting.

- You didn't drink enough water, so you get dehydrated.

- You have not learned how to play the sport in a way that keeps you from hurting yourself.

- You play a contact sport like hockey or football without wearing the pads and helmet that could protect you when you run into another player...or the goal post!

Here are some facts about injuries:

- Traumatic injuries include wounds that cause you to bleed, strains and sprains of ligaments and tendons, especially around the joints and broken bones.

When you bang into someone and your skin turns a dark color and becomes sensitive, that's a bruise or "contusion". Some of your small blood cells got damaged and are leaking under your skin.

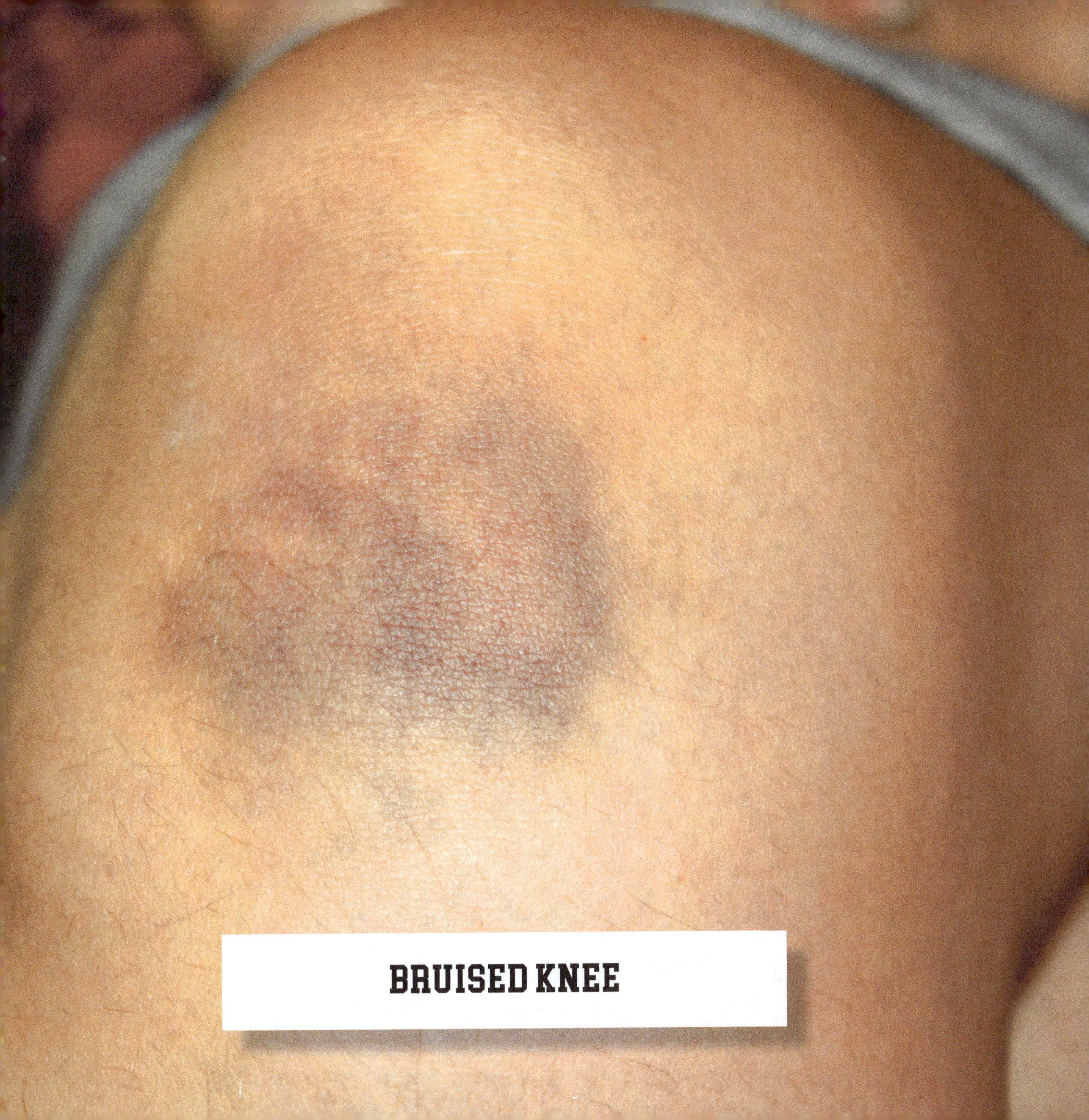
BRUISED KNEE

A catastrophic injury is one that hurts your head, brain, or spine.

- A chronic injury is one that, after you first hurt yourself, keeps coming back. Even if you are resting you may feel a dull pain, and there may be a swelling.

RUNNER'S KNEE

- Lots of people suffer concussions, the result of banging into something and bouncing your brain around in your skull. Concussions can be very serious, and their effects can last for years.

- "Runner's knee" is a chronic injury that people who run a lot may suffer. The cartilage between the bones of the knee joint becomes less able to act as a shock absorber.

Tennis Elbow

Right arm, lateral (outside) side

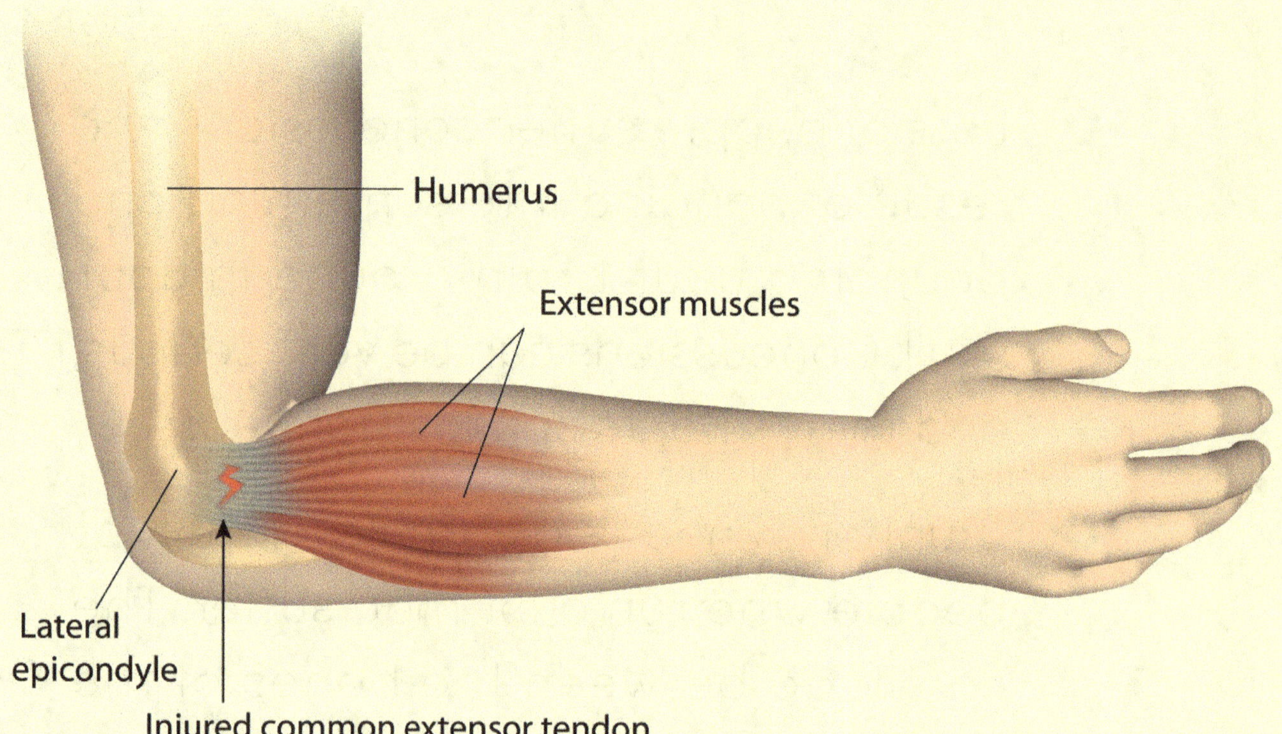

- "Tennis elbow" isn't just for tennis players. It is a chronic injury involving damage to the tendons of the elbow.

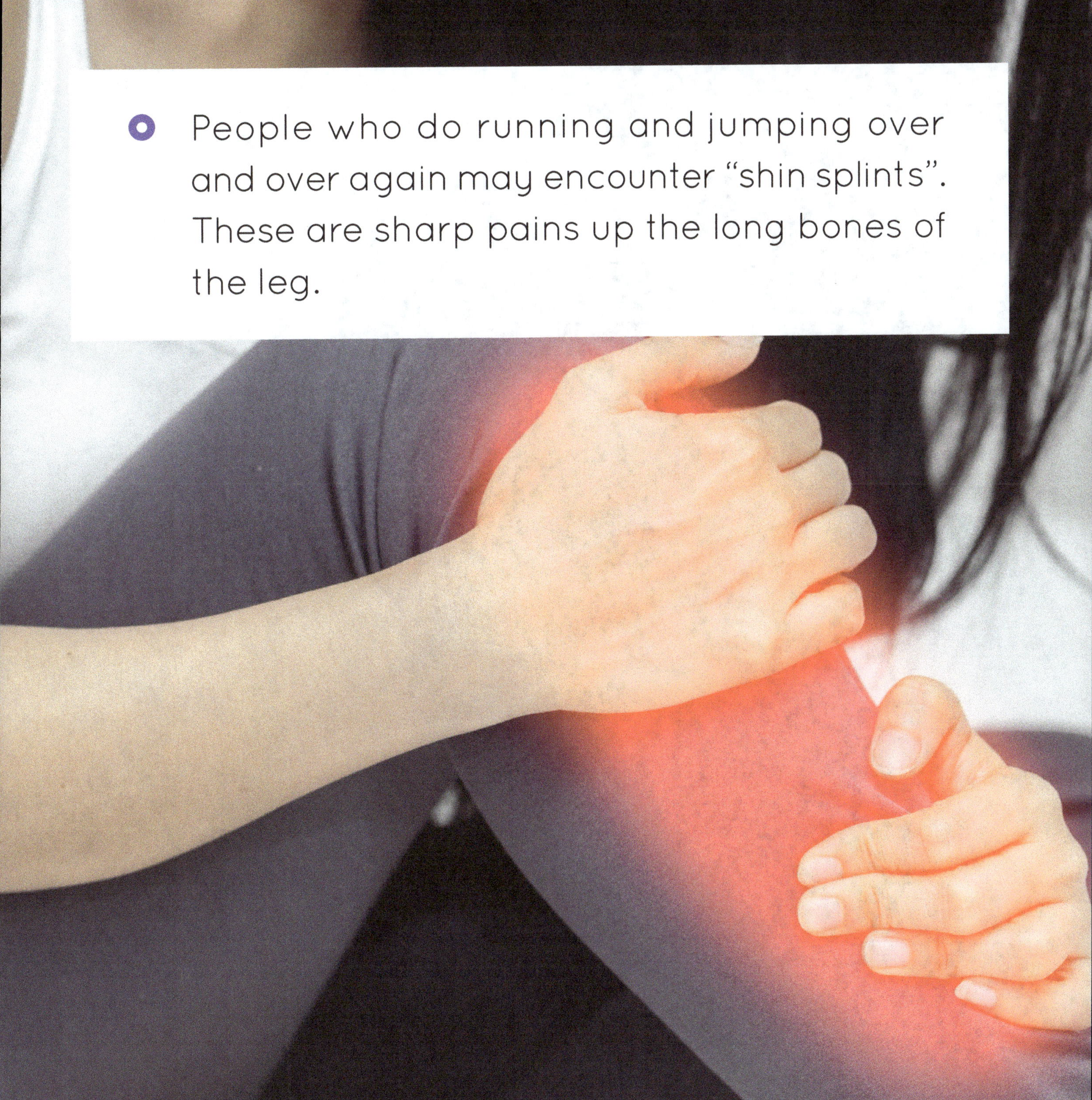
People who do running and jumping over
and over again may encounter "shin splints".
These are sharp pains up the long bones of
the leg.

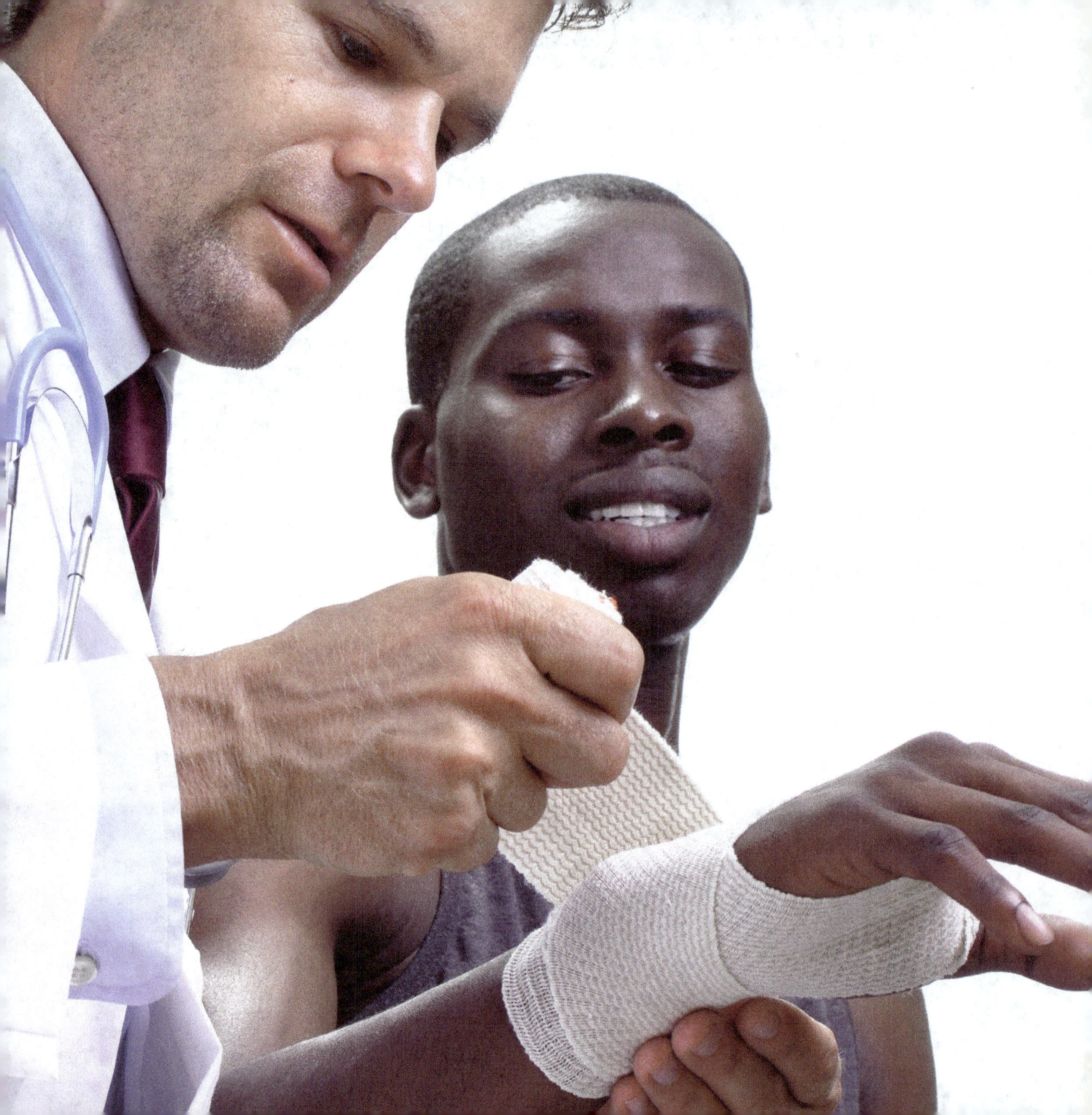

TREATING INJURIES

If you have banged your head or broken something, or have a bleeding injury that is more than a scrape, get trained medical help right away. This is nothing to fool around about!

If you do have a scrape or a cut that is too small to require a doctor's care, you still have work to do. Clean any dirt out of it with water, press on the wound to slow down any bleeding, and then cover it with a sterile dressing. Then leave it alone for a couple of days so it can start healing.

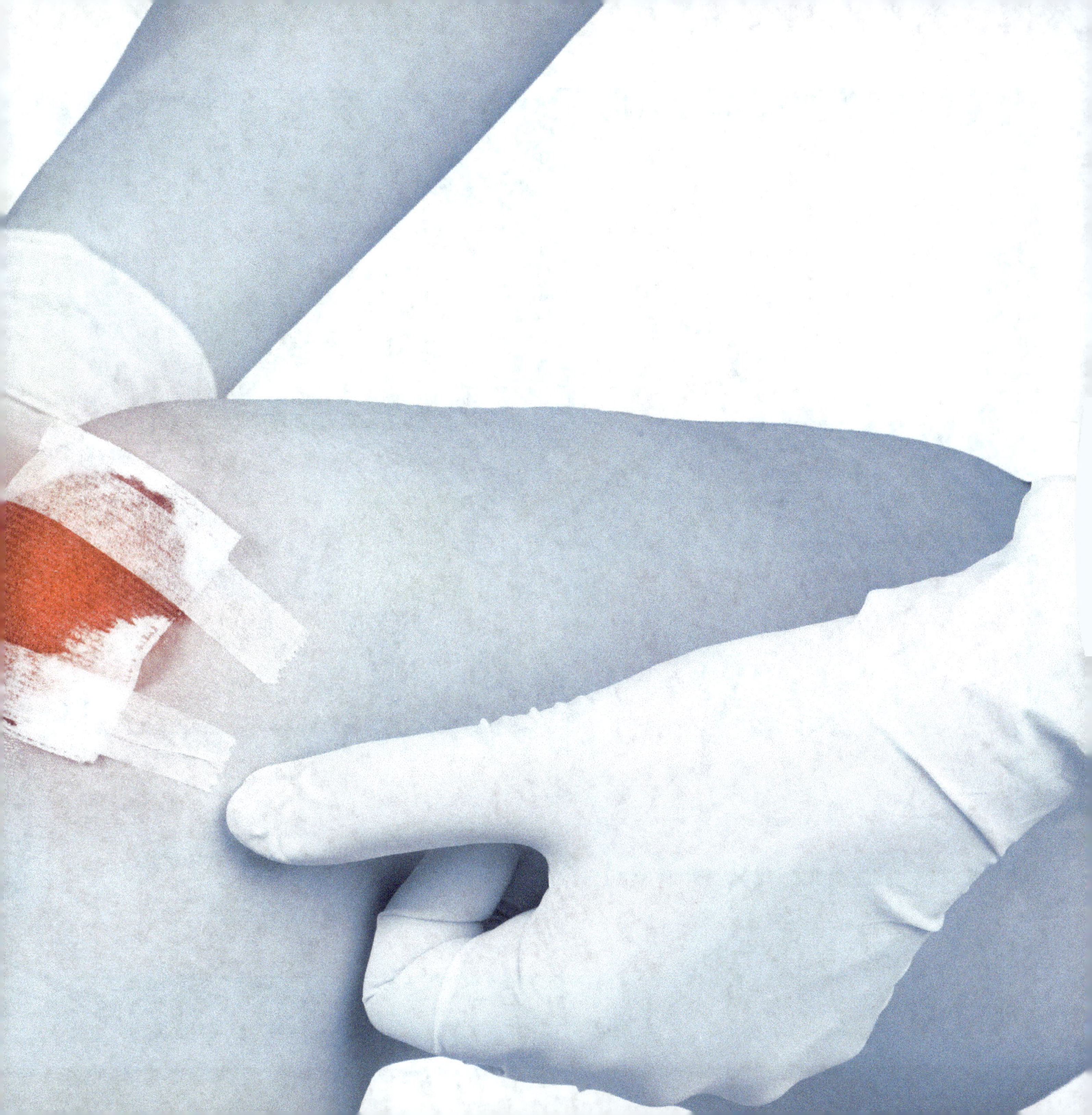

1. REST

SPRAINED ANKLE
TREATMENT
3. COMPRESSION

For sports injuries in general, remember RICE for what you do for the first 48 hours:

Rest
Ice
Compression
Elevation

Rest. Don't strain that part of your body any more.

Ice. Use an ice pack for twenty minutes every couple of hours to reduce swelling and pain.

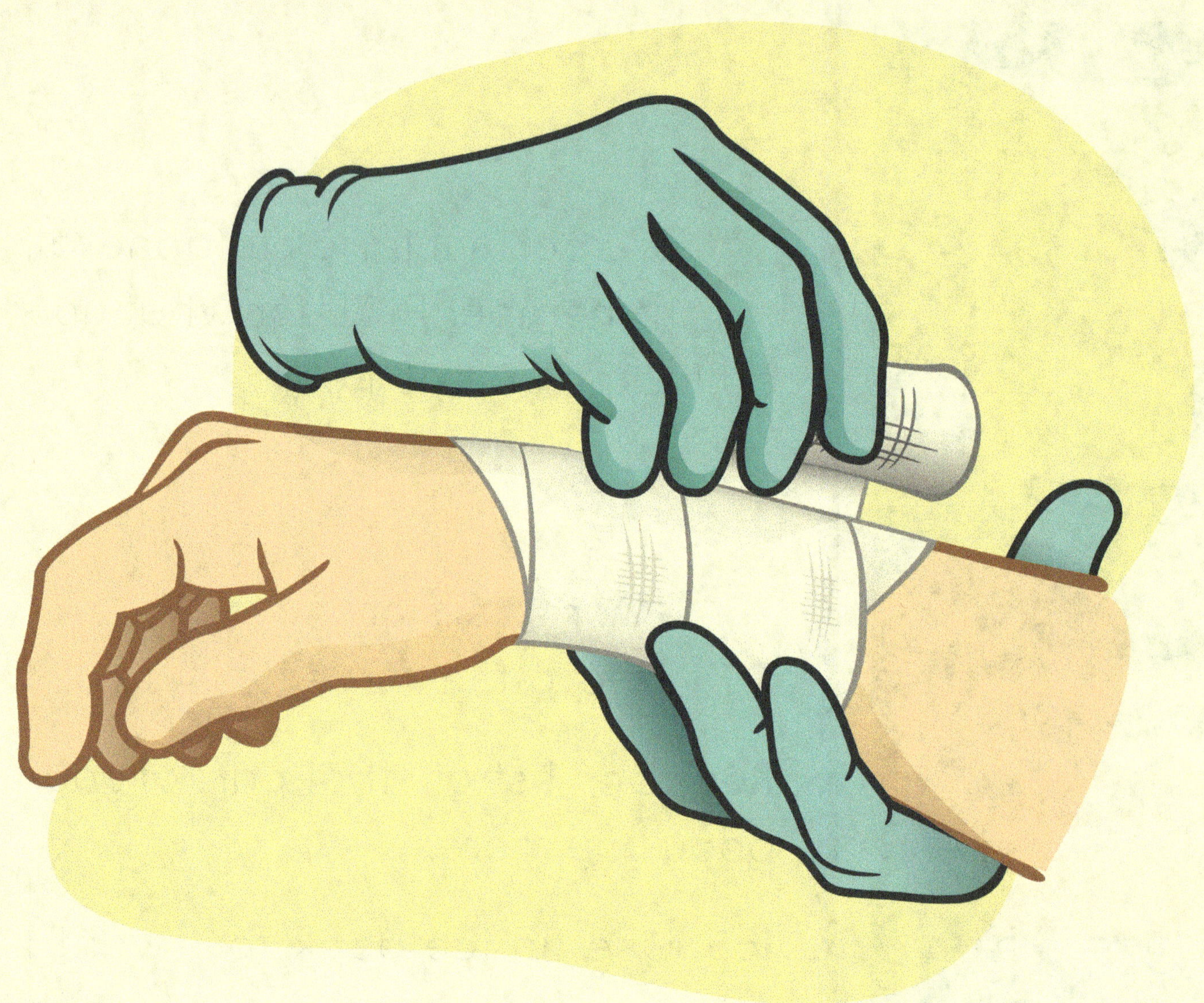

Compression: If it is a sprain, wrapping an elastic bandage around the joint will help keep you from irritating it more.

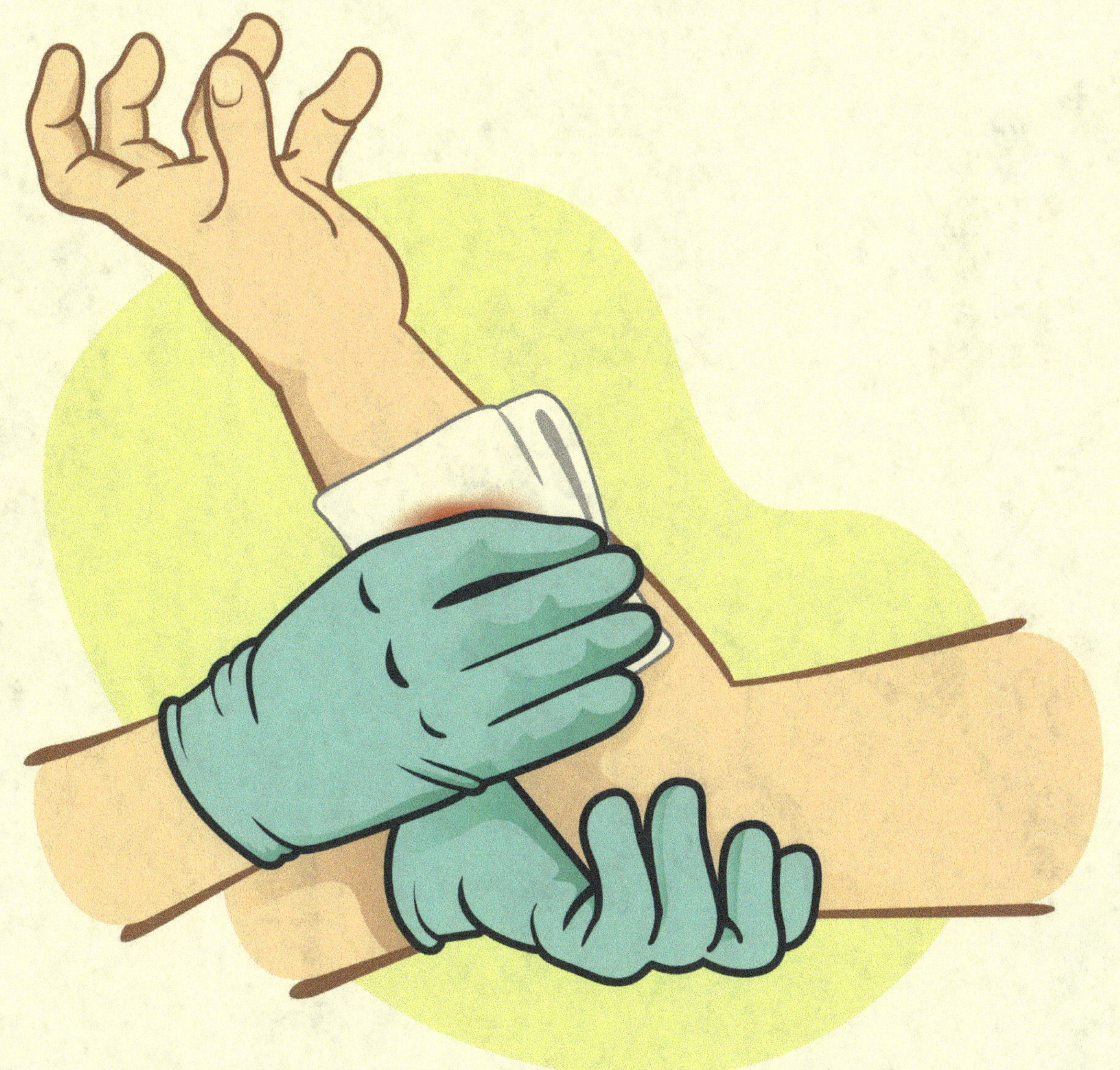

Elevation: Get the injured part higher than your heart, if possible. Take the weight off your leg, or rest your arm on a pillow, and let your body start healing!

For a problem that persists more than 48 hours, check with a medical professional. They may recommend medicine to reduce swelling, hot or cold packs, massage or even acupuncture to help the body recover. In extreme cases, like a broken bone, surgery may be necessary.

AN ACTIVE LIFE

Sports science shows us that leading an active life with lots of exercise will help us live longer and enjoy every day more. To learn about athletes who went further than that, read Baby Professor books like The Legends of Sports: Tiger Woods, Michael Jordan and Muhammad Ali and Women who Dominated in Sports.

Visit

BABY PROFESSOR
EDUCATION KIDS

www.BabyProfessorBooks.com

to download Free Baby Professor eBooks
and view our catalog of new and exciting
Children's Books